CHEWA

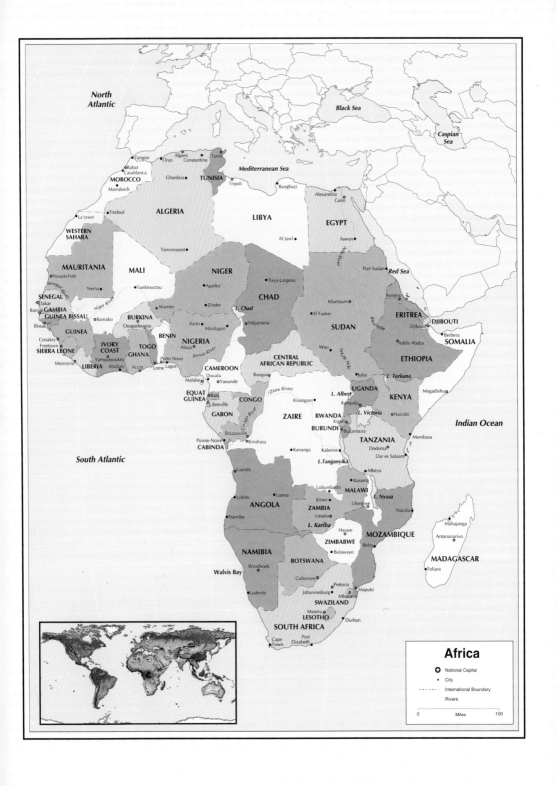

North
Atlantic

Black Sea

Caspian
Sea

Tangier
Oran Constantine Tunis
Rabat
Casablanca
MOROCCO
Ghardaia
Marrakech

Mediterranean Sea

TUNISIA
Tripoli
Banghazi

Alexandria
Cairo

La'youn Tindouf

ALGERIA

LIBYA

EGYPT

WESTERN
SAHARA

Al Jawf

Aswan

Tamanrasset

MAURITANIA

MALI

NIGER

Port Sudan Red Sea

Nouakchott

Nema Tombouctou

Agadez

CHAD

Faya-Largeau

Khartoum

Asmera
ERITREA
DJIBOUTI

Senegal River
SENEGAL
Dakar
Banjul GAMBIA
GUINEA BISSAU
Bissau

Niger River
Bamako

Niamey

Zinder
L. Chad
Kano

Maidugun

Ndjamena

El Fasher

SUDAN

Djibouti
Berbera
SOMALIA

BURKINA
Ouagadougou

BENIN
NIGERIA
Abuja

Wau

Addis Ababa

ETHIOPIA

Conakry
Freetown
SIERRA LEONE
Monrovia
LIBERIA

GUINEA
IVORY
COAST
Yamoussoukro
Abidjan

TOGO
GHANA
Accra
Lome Lagos

Benue River

Porto Novo

CAMEROON
Douala
Malabo Yaounde

CENTRAL
AFRICAN REPUBLIC

Bangui

Juba

L. Turkana

EQUAT
GUINEA Bata
Libreville

CONGO

(Zaire River)
Kisangani

UGANDA
L. Albert
Kampala

KENYA

Mogadishu

GABON

ZAIRE

RWANDA
Kigali
BURUNDI
Bujumbura

L. Victoria

Nairobi

Brazzaville
Pointe-Noire Kinshasa
CABINDA

Kananga

Kalemie

TANZANIA
Dodoma
Dar es Salaam

Mombasa

Indian Ocean

South Atlantic

Luanda

L.Tanganyika

Mbeya

Kasama

Lubumbashi

MALAWI
L. Nyasa

Lobito Luena
ANGOLA
Namibe

Kitwe
ZAMBIA
Lusaka
L. Kariba

Lilongwe

Nacala

Harare

MOZAMBIQUE

Mahajanga

Antananarivo

NAMIBIA

Walvis Bay
Windhoek

BOTSWANA

ZIMBABWE
Bulawayo

Belra

MADAGASCAR
Toliara

Luderitz

Gaborone

Pretoria
Johannesburg Maputo
Mbabane
SWAZILAND
Maseru
LESOTHO Durban

SOUTH AFRICA
Cape
Town Port
Elizabeth

Africa

✹ National Capital

• City

- - - International Boundary

Rivers

0   Miles   100

The Heritage Library of African Peoples

CHEWA

John Peffer-Engels, M.Phil.

THE ROSEN PUBLISHING GROUP, INC.
NEW YORK

Published in 1996 by The Rosen Publishing Group, Inc.
29 East 21st Street, New York, NY 10010

First Edition

Manufactured in the United States of America

Library of Congress Cataloging-in-Publication Data

Peffer-Engels, John, 1966–
    Chewa / John Peffer-Engels. — 1st ed.
      p. cm. — (The heritage library of African peoples)
    Includes bibliographical references and index.
    Summary: Presents the history, culture, art, and economics of the
Chewa people of Malawi, Zambia, and Mozambique.
    ISBN 0-8239-2010-0
    1. Chewa (African people)—Juvenile literature.   [1. Chewa
(African people)] I. Title. II. Series.
DT3192.C54P44   1996
968.97′004963918—dc20   96-7634
                                               CIP
                                               AC

Contents

INTRODUCTION

THERE IS EVERY REASON FOR US TO KNOW something about Africa and to understand its past and the way of life of its peoples. Africa is a rich continent that has for centuries provided the world with art, culture, labor, wealth, and natural resources. It has vast mineral deposits, fossil fuels, and commercial crops.

But perhaps most important is the fact that fossil evidence indicates that human beings originated in Africa. The earliest traces of human beings and their tools are almost two million years old. Their descendants have migrated throughout the world. To be human is to be of African descent.

The experiences of the peoples who stayed in Africa are as rich and as diverse as of those who established themselves elsewhere. This series of books describes their environment, their modes of subsistence, their relationships, and their customs and beliefs. The books present the variety of languages, histories, cultures, and religions that are to be found on the African continent. They demonstrate the historical linkages between African peoples and the way contemporary Africa has been affected by European colonial rule.

Africa is large, complex, and diverse. It encompasses an area of more than 11,700,000

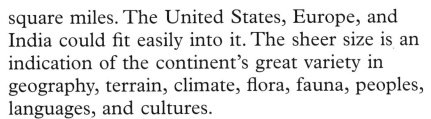

square miles. The United States, Europe, and India could fit easily into it. The sheer size is an indication of the continent's great variety in geography, terrain, climate, flora, fauna, peoples, languages, and cultures.

Much of contemporary Africa has been shaped by European colonial rule, industrialization, urbanization, and the demands of a world economic system. For more than seventy years, large regions of Africa were ruled by Great Britain, France, Belgium, Portugal, and Spain. African peoples from various ethnic, linguistic, and cultural backgrounds were brought together to form colonial states.

For decades Africans struggled to gain their independence. It was not until after World War II that the colonial territories became independent African states. Today, almost all of Africa is ruled by Africans. Large numbers of Africans live in modern cities. Rural Africa is also being transformed, and yet its people still engage in many of their customs and beliefs.

Contemporary circumstances and natural events have not always been kind to ordinary Africans. Today, however, new popular social movements and technological innovations pose great promise for future development.

George C. Bond, Ph.D., Director
Institute of African Studies
Columbia University, New York

The history of the Chewa people dates back at least 800 years. Today, they live mostly in the modern country of Malawi. This boy plays contemporary music on the guitar he has made. It uses an oil can for the resonator, or sound box.

chapter

1

THE PEOPLE

TODAY THE CHEWA NUMBER OVER ONE million. Most live in the central area of Malawi and nearby regions of Mozambique and Zambia. Some live and work in modern cities such as Lilongwe, the capital of Malawi.

Language, culture, geography, and historical struggles for political power all play a role in defining who the Chewa are.

Chewa history dates back to at least 1200 AD, when related peoples migrated from what is now Zaire. Three centuries later they had developed a trading network that extended to the Indian Ocean. They were known to the Portuguese and the Swahili-speaking peoples on the coast as the Maravi (pronounced maravwee), after whom Lake Malawi is named.

The Chewa today are related in history, culture, and language to other Maravi groups. These groups include the Mang'anja, Nyanja, Nsenga,

Chipeta, Zimba, and Mbo peoples of southern Malawi and western Mozambique.

Ancestors of the modern Chewa eventually settled just south and west of Lake Malawi. In the 1800s, they were described to Portuguese explorers by locals as *Ceva*, meaning "strangers." Since Malawi's independence from Great Britain in 1964, the government of Hastings Banda has tried to identify the nation of Malawi only with those who speak the Chewa language and are part of the Chewa culture. However, Malawi includes people of many different ethnic backgrounds. Chewa culture has been used as a symbol of pride. It has also been used as a political tool to suppress other groups in Malawi, such as the Ngoni, Yao, and Tumbuka, whose traditions and politics differ from the government's.▲

Lake Malawi is the main geographical feature of Malawi.

chapter

2

VILLAGE LIFE

MOST CHEWA TODAY LIVE IN SMALL FARMING villages in the highlands west and south of Lake Malawi. They continue many of the traditions that date back to the Maravi period. However, many traditional chiefs in Africa have lost their political power to the governments of modern African states. In Malawi, the political organization of society has changed a great deal in the last one hundred fifty years. Chewa chiefs still lead fertility festivities and initiation ceremonies for the village youth. In traditional, rural society, elders are greatly respected, and family relationships are considered very important.

▼ THE LAND ▼

The region connecting Zambia, Mozambique, and Malawi, where most Chewa live, varies greatly in climate and landscape. It is considered

11

Malawi is a very beautiful country. Seen here are fishermen, paddling their dugout canoe along the shore of Lake Malawi. The large trees are baobabs.

some of the most beautiful country in Africa.

The hot plains near the shore of Lake Malawi are bordered by steep hills and cliffs, which lead to a hilly plateau. Streams drain from the highlands toward Lake Malawi in the east, toward the Zambezi River in the south, and to the Luangwa River in the north. The high plateau is mostly woodland, with grassy savanna valleys. Climate differs greatly, depending on the landscape.

Yearly temperatures average between 70 degrees and 80 degrees, with winter frosts occurring in the mountains. Hot days reach over 100 degrees in the valleys. The summer rainy season lasts from November to April. For the rest of the year it is very dry, and spontaneous fires often burn across the land.

▼ FOOD ▼

Hunting was once important to the Chewa, but today great herds are remembered only in folk tales. Today, antelope, zebra, elephant, hippopotamus, lion, leopard, civet cat, jackal, monkey, anteater, and other smaller animals are found only in small numbers or in game reserves. Wild pigs, baboons, and hyenas are still fairly common pests that occasionally destroy crops or kill livestock. Turtles, chameleons, snakes, and crocodiles are common in Chewa country.

The fish in Lake Malawi are important for food and trade. These small fish are usually dried on platforms like those seen behind the children.

Lake Malawi is 350 miles long. It is one of the many huge African lakes that formed in the Great Rift Valley. This valley is an enormous tear in the continent that occurred in prehistoric times.

Lake Malawi is a plentiful source of fish, with more than 200 tropical varieties. Some of these fish are unique and many are beautifully colored. Fish, either cooked or dried, is an important source of protein (and flavor) in the local diet.

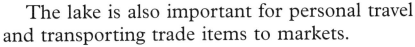

The lake is also important for personal travel and transporting trade items to markets.

The cattle kept in Chewa villages are considered "insurance" in case of drought, or as a luxury food to be eaten on special occasions.

In the highlands there are many wide shallow valleys, called *malambo*. These grassy *malambo* fill with water during the wet season, providing excellent grazing for livestock and fertile soil for small vegetable gardens.

Just before the rains each year, the Chewa set their dry fields on fire. These fires clear the ground for the next year's crop and fertilize the soil with ash. The symbolism of fire, rain, and fertility is central to Chewa belief.

The everyday food of the Chewa was once sorghum, a tough, drought-resistant grain that was cooked into a porridge, like grits. Maize has since replaced sorghum as the grain of choice. It is pounded and boiled into a thick porridge called *nsima*, which is stirred until stiff and slightly moist to the touch. This is eaten by taking a handful and rolling it into a ball, then dipping it in a hot spicy relish or stew, called *ndiwo*. *Ndiwo* is a part of every Chewa meal. Each person has their own recipe for *ndiwo*. Home-grown ingredients may include pumpkin leaves and flowers, beans, and chili peppers. Occasionally some meat or fish is added.

Other vegetables grown by the Chewa include

sweet potatoes, cucumbers, various squashes, and groundnuts. Fruit trees are also an important source of food. Mango trees are especially valued, and it is illegal to cut them down. The Chewa also collect wild plants and roots from the bush. These are used to make *ndiwo* or to cure illness. Wild herbs are also used for making charms to protect people and property from harm.

▼ FARMING ▼

English missionaries discovered the Chewa and their neighbors had extensive knowledge of soil types and farming methods. One traveler in the 1800s was asked why he was going to Africa. He replied that he intended to teach the Africans agriculture. But when he got to Africa, he realized that Africans knew more about farming than he did.

The Chewa practice crop rotation, the planting of different crops from year to year, and grow certain plants together, such as maize and beans. These techniques allow the Chewa to grow successful crops on the same small patch of land for many years, without the use of fertilizers. To protect their seeds from wild animals, the Chewa have been known to plant three or more maize seeds in the same hole. This allows "one for the wild pig, one for the guinea fowl, and one for ourselves." Fields are protected against

Large farming businesses now occupy most of the best land in Malawi. These men are picking tea leaves.

theft by using spiritual herbs and medicines that cause sickness to thieves.

Even on rich soil, farming is long and difficult work. It makes up an important part of the daily routine, and it holds an important place in the worldview of most rural Chewa. The coming of the rains and the ongoing fertility of the land are vital concerns for them. Drought is common in the region. During January and February, when food from the past year is running low, the Chewa often barter goats and chickens with their neighbors for grain.

In the past, when the soil was exhausted from many seasons of planting, entire small villages would move to a new site nearby. There they would set up new houses and begin to farm. Today large farming businesses have taken up most of the land. Here single cash crops, such as tea, coffee, tobacco, and cotton, are grown for export. Because land is now scarce, soil erosion and poor crop returns have become serious problems for local farmers.

After the harvest, around July, there is little to do in the fields and gardens until the next rain. Villagers use this time to celebrate annual ceremonies, repair their houses, and go on journeys to visit relatives and friends.

▼ VILLAGES ▼

Chewa villages sometimes contain over one hundred people and usually consist of members of one or more extended families. The number of houses can reach sixty or more in a village and these are clustered irregularly in groups. Large trees are left standing for shade during the heat of the day.

Each married woman has her own house, where she lives with her children. Young bachelors live in simple huts away from their mothers' houses. Many large storage containers stand on stilts to protect their contents against pests. Peanuts are stored in structures with earthen walls and thatched roofs. Corn is stored in large vessels of woven bamboo, which allow the flow of air to keep the corn dry.

Traditionally styled houses are round. They are constructed of a wide circle of wooden posts that are plastered with thick mud. This is covered with hard, black clay and painted in a lighter color with geometric patterns, birds, and human figures. Roofs are made by thatching reeds onto a cone-shaped framework. The roof is then placed onto the drum shape formed by the earthen walls. The roof extends beyond the walls, forming a shady area. Additional posts help support the roof.

When women cook inside the houses, smoke rises up through the thatched roofs. The smoke blackens the roof with soot and keeps insects away.

Today, many rural houses, particularly those belonging to wealthy people, are built in a rectangular, Western style. They are constructed of brick or concrete and often have flat roofs made of corrugated metal. These kinds of houses, together with large hotels, office blocks, and administration buildings, fill the larger towns.

▼ CRAFT SPECIALISTS ▼

When the harvest has been gathered, people focus on making crafts. Excellent craftspersons may receive requests for their work from outside their own village.

During the days of the Maravi, the Chewa dug iron ore from the earth and smelted it in

Today, many kinds of buildings are found in Malawi. Tailors often work outside small rural stores (above). In the cities (below), Malawians have a wide variety of occupations, similar to towns anywhere in the world.

KNOWLEDGE AND SECRECY

For the Chewa, being "in-the-know," *adziwa*, brings status. Elders know the deeper meanings of songs and proverbs and the secret workings of things.

Through initiation ceremonies, young people come to understand the meaning of Chewa customs. Initiates are taught *mwambo*, secret information.

Craft-making skill, or *nzelu* (meaning wisdom, or know-how), is usually passed down within a family. One can have *nzelu* for basket making, hunting, healing, or other kinds of specialist activity. The word *nzelu* implies an almost magical knowledge of "how to do" something.

furnaces. Then their blacksmiths fashioned it into beautiful and useful iron implements such as hoes, axes, arrowheads, and knives. Today blacksmiths use scrap iron and steel to repair bicycles, sewing machines, and guns.

Pottery and basketry have been practiced by the Chewa for centuries, both locally and for outside trade. These traditional crafts have become very popular among European tourists. More recently, wooden sculptures and ornately carved items of everyday use, such as chairs and candlesticks, have been made for sale.

▼ WORK ▼

Most chores in a Chewa village are done by

BEER BREWING

The Chewa have a reputation as great beer brewers. The women make a mixture from sprouted corn or sorghum called *mowa*. This nourishing and mildly alcoholic beverage, drunk by both men and women, is served at social gatherings. *Mowa* is given to people in a village who come together to help work on a family farm or build a house. If the women of the house are known to make delicious beer, more people will be willing to join the work party. A group that helps a family with its farming is called *mowa wolima*, meaning the "beer of hoeing."

women. However, both women and men prepare the family gardens. This is the most important work of the household. Women fetch wood and water and prepare meals. They are also responsible for raising children. Men cut down trees to clear fields for planting and build storage containers for crops and livestock pens. Men construct the supports for houses, and women plaster the walls and floors and paint the outside with designs. Children weed the gardens and catch field mice, which they like to cook as snacks.

In the 1800s, the Western economic system was forced upon the Chewa. This has placed new pressures on the traditional roles of men and women in Chewa society. British administrators demanded that Africans pay taxes. In order to earn cash, Africans were forced to work for the colonists at very low wages. Since the beginning of this century, many Chewa men have become migrant laborers. They have gone to Rhodesia (now Zimbabwe) and South Africa to work on farms, in mines and factories, or as servants. Sometimes they are gone for years or never return. Women, children, and older men are left to do the work of keeping up the gardens and houses.

Today, cash is required for school fees, clothes, medicines, tools, and other items. There are few ways in the village to make enough money to cover these costs. Many people leave the rural areas hoping to find a better life in the towns and cities. ▲

Women do most of the household chores. This young woman uses a pestle to pound grain in the mortar.

chapter

3

SOCIETY

HUMAN RELATIONSHIPS ARE CENTRAL TO
Chewa society and daily life in Chewa villages.
Most important are a person's relationships with
his or her immediate family, with other relatives,
with other families in the village, and within the
network of families that are united under a par-
ticular chiefdom.

▼ WOMEN AND THE LINEAGE ▼
Women have a special place in Chewa
society and belief. They are recognized as repro-
ducers of the lineage, an extended family of
people related to the same ancestor. The Chewa
are matrilineal, meaning that they inherit rights
to property and land through their mothers.
Matrilineal societies also trace their family back
to a female ancestor.
Large lineages, such as the Banda or Phiri

families, have members in many different villages. Lineages are divided into about four generations, from the oldest living grandmother to the youngest children. In these extended families, members work the gardens together, share food, and assist each other with daily chores. Wealthy and powerful lineages attract new members, who then "claim" common ancestry and become members of the family.

The head of a lineage helps to settle disputes between members and is in charge of distributing land given by the headman of the village. The lineage head is usually its oldest living female ancestor or one of her brothers.

A lineage is called *mbele*, which means "descended from the same breast." The children of one mother, or all the descendants of one female, make up an *mbumba*, a family of dependents. Elder brothers are called *nkhoswe*, guardians of the women of the lineage. They are consulted on all important issues, such as marriage, divorce, and inheritance.

When a young man is old enough to become guardian of his sisters, he may wish to escape the authority of his mother's brother. He may choose to leave the village or the family homestead, taking his sisters and their children with him. Grandmothers, who give their property, social status, and name to their granddaughters, often move with their sons and daughters to

form a new village or a new area within the same village.

▼ MARRIAGE ▼

In Chewa society the most important family relationship is between a mother and her *nkhoswe*, or male guardian. The role of the husband is less important. As a rule, a man or woman must marry someone from a different lineage. When two people wish to marry, the *nkhoswe* from both families meet to decide if it is a good match. Women are married young, around age twelve to fourteen, and to older men.

Traditionally, a man lives with his wife and her family in their village for several years after marriage. He is regarded as a stranger to his wife's family. His home is considered to be in his own village, with his own family. Husbands have little power or respect in the new village. The young husband is expected to build a house for his new wife, to work in the garden of his parents-in-law, and to make craft items for them.

After several years, a husband may earn the respect of his in-laws as a father of many children, as a hard worker, and as one who has developed a good knowledge of village affairs. Then he may ask to pay a small fee to his wife's family in order to move with her and their children to his own village. Only if he is a village headman, lineage guardian, or chief, may a man ask his wife to live with him in his own village from the start of their marriage. A husband has no rights of ownership over his children or his wife's family's property. If a man leaves the village without his wife, or if he dies, his children are taken in by his wife's brother. Historians claim that divorce was very common and relatively easy among the Chewa.

▼ SOCIAL CHANGES ▼

Several factors have changed traditional family structures. Some changes have been unfavorable for women.

During the slave trade in the 1800s, lineage heads sometimes bought slaves as wives for young men in the family. Slave wives had no "home" village, so their husbands could remain in their own village, have rights over their children, and increase the wealth and property of their own lineage head, rather than contribute to the village of their wife.

After the turn of this century, Christian missionaries encouraged couples to form Western-style nuclear families. In these families, the husband is the "head of the household" and a couple is protected by God rather than by the family elders. With British rule and the rise of Western education, the position of the husband was emphasized. The authority of *nkhoswe*, head-

WOMEN

In modern Malawi, women have fewer opportunities than men for education, government positions, and wage labor. More than 90 percent of women live in rural areas. Thirty percent of rural women are heads of households. The many hours women spend running the family and working in gardens partly explains their difficulty in finding other employment. Since the introduction of "customary law," it has become hard for women to improve their situation, because simply leaving their villages or divorcing their husbands is now harder to do. In the past, women were protected by their male relatives (nkhoswe). Now they are controlled by the new, so-called "traditional powers" of their husbands and chiefs.

Dr. Banda created the League of Malawi Women in 1958 as an extension of his Malawi Congress Party (MCP). The League raised money for its activities through a monopoly on the sale of African beer, mowa. Prominent League members, those in political favor with Banda, and those who could afford to buy a League uniform performed traditional dances and praise songs at Banda's official appearances.

The President called the League his mbumba, implying that these women were members of his family.

men, and chiefs over children and property was undermined. Mission-educated teachers and civil servants moved their wives and children to posts far away from traditional family guardians.

The rise in the number of migrant laborers has further changed Chewa society. Exposure to the customs of other people and the possibility of escaping from the authority of their wives'

The League of Malawi Women supported President Banda. Here a League member, wearing fabric printed with Banda's face, assists Dr. Banda at an official opening.

Many Chewa men migrate to cities in Malawi and elsewhere. This man operates a small store selling kerosene.

parents has led some men to abandon the old marriage customs. Labor migrancy has created tensions between the sexes, because men fear their wives will find another man while they are away. Chewa women feel abandoned by their working husbands. Migrant husbands prefer to have their wives supervised by having them live with the husband's family while they are away.

Many Chewa today still believe that it is ideal to follow the traditional Chewa family pattern and its customs, even though circumstances have changed so much in the last century. Most Chewa still marry within a few miles of their home village.▲

chapter

4

TRADITIONAL POLITICS

TRADITIONAL POLITICAL AUTHORITIES IN
Chewa society lost most of their power over
people and land during the colonial period and
under later African governments.

In the past, rivalries within chiefdoms could
be solved by simply forming new chiefdoms.
This is no longer possible in Malawi, because
the number of chiefdoms was frozen by the
government after independence.

In Malawi today, rural Chewa can still bring
family or property disputes to their village
headman or regional chief. They can also take
their case to a government court. Today traditional chiefs serve more administrative func-
tions in their communities than before, such as
recording births and deaths and collecting
taxes.

However, chiefs still have important spiritual and moral roles in their communities.

▼ THE *MFUMU* ▼

The village headman (*mfumu*), usually male but sometimes a woman, is frequently the head of the largest lineage in the village. The *mfumu* distributes land among the various family guardians, or *nkhoswe*, in the village. The *mfumu* also ensures that village affairs run smoothly.

When a child is born, the people say, "Rejoice, a new *mfumu* has been born!" for it is said that any good person has the potential to become a *mfumu*. The *mfumu* is considered a fair and wise judge of disputes, a person of great calm and dignity, and one who is never out of line. An *mfumu* should be a generous host.

▼ THE *MWINI DZIKO* ▼

Above the level of the village headmen there are regional chiefs, or *mwini dziko*, and paramount chiefs. Village chiefs owe tribute (gifts of food and other goods) to the regional chiefs who control the many villages in the territory.

The *mwini dziko* installs a new headman when one dies. He settles arguments between villages and assures the fertility of the land by performing special ceremonies. The regional chief presides over the initiation of girls and boys into adulthood at Cinamwali and Nyau

Society ceremonies, which are also closely related to the prosperity of the land. In the past, the *mwini dziko* also assembled large armies.

▼ PARAMOUNT CHIEFS ▼

Historically, the Chewa had few paramount chiefs. They were direct descendants of the Kalonga, the first Maravi ruler in the Lake Malawi region during the 1400s. The paramount chiefs each controlled a large territory and received tribute from the regional chiefs. Paramounts were regarded as having great spiritual power, which they used to protect their subjects, promote fertility and order, ward off disease, and appeal to the supreme God, Mulungu, for rain.

Paramounts chiefs were "guardians of fire." It is said that Paramount Chief Undi kept a fire burning in his house day and night, fueled by pieces of the mats that girls had sat upon during their initiation into womanhood. These mats were an important item of tribute.

When a paramount chief died, the royal fire was extinguished and people ran about madly in the streets until the next leader was installed in office. For the Chewa, even today, the order and well-being of the country are connected to ideas about rulership, fire, fertility, and rain. All of these ideas are combined in the chief's symbolic control of fire.▲

Regional chiefs oversee ceremonies, such as initiations and masquerades. Seen here (above) is an initiate being led back to her village of Nzengwe, in Zambia. At the masquerade below, a ceremonial fire burns. Paramount chiefs are associated with fire.

chapter

5

THE MARAVI EMPIRE

SOME CHEWA TODAY BELIEVE THAT THE hill named Kaphirintiwa in central Malawi is a sacred place, because it is the site of creation. In the stone can be seen footprints of humans and animals. There are also marks believed to have been made by the first farming tools that fell from heaven. Kaphirintiwa is the site of an important rain shrine. It is also near the place where the early Chewa people first settled.

According to oral history and myth, the people now known as Chewa originated in the Congo, near Lake Mweru. Around 1400 AD, Chief Chinkhole Phiri and his mother led their followers to the area south and west of Lake Malawi. Here they met up with earlier migrants from the Congo. The Chewa claimed that the earlier migrants were related to Chewa ancestors, so they intermarried with them and made them part of the Chewa society.

They also found hunting and gathering peoples of very short stature called Kafula, who had been in the region since at least 1500 BC. These Kafula fought to keep the Chewa off their land, but they were driven south across the Zambezi River.

By the 1500s the Phiri were the paramount family. They ruled over several semi-independent chiefdoms in the eastern part of Central Africa. The Phiri were known as the Maravi, or "fire flames." They controlled trade in fine cloth, ivory, foodstuffs, iron goods, craft items, salt, slaves, and precious metals. They also traded with other African peoples and with Portuguese and Arab traders working along the Zambezi River and the Indian Ocean. This linked the Maravi into a network of African trade that reached to Asia, Europe, and the Americas. All trade with outsiders had to pass through the royal capital.

The Maravi received tribute from their people. They used some of it to trade with foreigners. From the carcass of every killed elephant, the tusk that lay upon the ground and "touched the king's land" was taken to the regional chief, who passed it on to the paramount chief. He could trade it for cloth or slaves with a trader. Hunters also took to their chiefs items of religious significance, such as the red feathers of certain birds and the skins of lions and leopards. The poison parts of animals were also given to the chief, because only he was considered immune to their lethal power. These poisons were then distributed to hunters to tip their arrows.

Maravi rulers could call up large armies from among their chiefdoms. These armies dominated a large area east, west, and south of Lake Malawi. Rulers strengthened their hold over conquered people by marrying their women. They also exchanged sisters with the royal families of defeated groups. Since ownership of property and the right to become a chief were handed down from mothers to their children, such marriages gave the Maravi power and property among those they conquered. In effect, the Maravi become members of the family.

The paramount chief made the final decision about disputes that lesser chiefs were unable to solve. However, most government responsibilities remained in the hands of local leaders.

Much of the wealth of the Maravi, just as for the Chewa today, came from farming. The earth in their country was very fertile, and local farmers often produced surpluses for trade. Land was considered precious. Paramounts distributed land among local chiefs who, in turn, allocated it to village headmen. Food and other goods were stored to help the poor, to give as gifts to loyal local leaders, to entertain visitors,

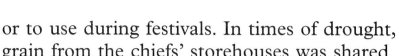

or to use during festivals. In times of drought, grain from the chiefs' storehouses was shared with the people.

▼ THE DECLINE OF THE MARAVI ▼

The Maravi federation was at its peak during the 1600s, but experts disagree about how powerful it was. As the federation grew, it became difficult to control the more distant territories. Paramount chiefs began to run out of land to give to new chiefs. Competition for trade and the invasion of new groups into the region combined to break down Maravi power.

By the 1700s, the Maravi federation had broken into rival chiefdoms. The Chewa are a core group that separated from the Maravi. In the 1700s, individual chiefs preferred to deal directly with Portuguese and Muslim traders in their area, rather than share the wealth with their paramount chief. The Portuguese conquered large areas for their own estates, called *prazos*, along the Zambezi River. They also employed local hunters to hunt for ivory on Maravi land. In an act of resistance, the paramount chief Undi closed down his small gold mines so that the Portuguese traders would stay out of his territory. Nonetheless, by 1780 the head of a leading Portuguese family had married one of Chief Undi's daughters. According to the Maravi matrilineal system, this meant that the

Portuguese man's son became part of the Maravi royal family.

In weakened form, the power of the Maravi continued into the 1800s.

▼ THE SLAVE TRADE ▼

Maravi rulers "sold off" disobedient subjects to slavers. They bought slaves as wives for loyal chiefs. As the Maravi Empire declined, slave hunters from the east coast of Africa began to capture slaves in Maravi territory. Slave hunters chose this area because they had already taken many slaves from the east coast. At the same time there was an increased demand for slaves in Arabia, Egypt, and the Persian Gulf.

The slave trade had a devastating effect on African societies and their relationships with their neighbors. The Yao people lived to the east and south of Lake Malawi and had mostly become Muslim. They acted as middlemen in the trade between the Indian Ocean and the Maravi. By the 1800s, they had become specialists in slaving and were armed with guns.

From the 1830s on, the region was invaded by waves of warlike Ngoni peoples who were fleeing the rule of Shaka, the Zulu king in South Africa. The Ngoni were a herding people, unlike the agricultural Chewa. They were organized into the military system developed by Shaka Zulu. They moved northward, raiding villages, until they reached Malawi and Tanzania. They forced the young men of the people they conquered, including the Chewa, to join their army.

At first, the Chewa welcomed the Yao as protectors against the invading Ngoni. But the Yao slave traders began to capture slaves from Chewa territory.

So the Chewa began to befriend the Ngoni, because their military efficiency was useful in fighting off Yao slave traders. In the 1850s a Ngoni splinter group, called the Maseko Ngoni, settled among the Chewa. The Ngoni forced the Chewa to adopt the dress, fighting techniques, dances, and marriage rules of the Ngoni. Eventually the Ngoni adopted the Chewa language and some Chewa customs.

The British put an end to slavery in 1890. This was a great relief to many African societies, which had been severely disrupted by the curse of slavery. It signaled the beginning of a new period of troubles: the era of English domination.▲

chapter

6

COLONIZATION

DAVID LIVINGSTONE TRAVELED TO THE LAKE Malawi region between 1858 and 1863. He sent reports about the ravages of the slave trade back to England. He encouraged the British to take control of the region and stop the trade. Several generations of Scottish and other missionaries followed him. They laid the groundwork for colonial domination by converting Africans to Christianity and strongly encouraging the introduction of Western ways.

The missionaries had little success before World War II. They were viewed as a threat to Chewa values. Mission schools were seen to be in direct competition with Chewa initiation schools for control of young men and women.

By the 1890s, Chewa land was under the control of the British Central Africa Protectorate. Using the abolition of slavery as its

Many missionaries tried to convert Malawians. At first they met much resistance. Mission schools have, however, educated many Malawians.

justification for occupying the region, Britain remained in control until 1964. Chewa leader Mwase Kasungu led a failed attempt to resist the British, finally committing suicide in 1896. The Nyau Society, a secret men's organization, united the people against the Christian missions and against the chiefs appointed by the British. Nyau was banned by the British, but it continued to operate in secret.

Unlike other English colonies, the area around Lake Malawi attracted few settlers. It had little mineral wealth, and Europeans thought that the climate was unsuitable. Still, the Lake itself was a strategic possession.

The English took control of the appointment

of chiefs, according to their policy of indirect rule. Indirect rule meant that the British used chiefs to do what the British wanted, such as performing unpopular tasks like collecting tax. In the 1920s, the British turned what they regarded as Chewa traditions and customs into "customary law." The British rearranged Chewa traditions of authority to suit themselves. Headmen were given more power, matching territorial chiefs' powers. Some minor chiefs liked their new powers, which enabled them to profit from women's beer brewing and migrants' wages.

▼ HUT TAX ▼

In Malawi and many other African countries, the British demanded "hut tax." Every house had to pay a tax. This forced Africans to begin to earn cash. The Chewa economic system had never involved cash. It depended on families farming for the food they needed and trading their surpluses for other items. This way of life could not continue when the British demanded "hut tax." Those unable to pay their taxes were forced to work under brutal conditions on British estates. Conditions were even worse under the Portuguese in neighboring Mozambique. As a result, thousands of refugees entered Malawi.

When men went away to work, the farms at home often no longer produced enough food to

The extended family plays an important role in the lives of most Malawians. Since colonization, many family customs have changed a great deal.

feed the family. Then more cash was needed to buy food. The desire for Western products also created a need for cash.

Many Africans recognized that the "hut tax" was not unlike slavery: it forced Africans to work for others against their will. Rebellions in English-speaking colonies over the "hut tax" were brutally suppressed by the British.

▼LABOR AND LAND▼

Under British control in the late 1800s, the economy of the Malawi region turned away from the old African trade networks. It was drawn into the mining industry in South Africa, which was also a British colony at the time. By 1903, labor recruiters from South Africa were taking

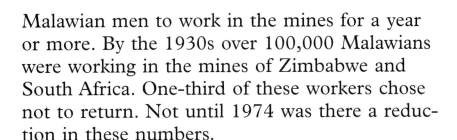

Malawian men to work in the mines for a year or more. By the 1930s over 100,000 Malawians were working in the mines of Zimbabwe and South Africa. One-third of these workers chose not to return. Not until 1974 was there a reduction in these numbers.

One result of labor migrancy was that a serious labor shortage developed on the family farms back home. Traditional social discipline went into decline. Migrant laborers increasingly relied on "customary law" to take control of property out of the hands of women.

Unlike their neighbors, the Chewa were little affected by either white settlers or labor migrancy at first. They lived on fertile soil and sold their surplus food to pay taxes. However, Africans were forced to work as porters for the British campaign in Africa during World War I. Food was demanded for the army. This caused an even greater shortage of people to work on the Chewa farms, and a scarcity of food. The duty to feed the colonial labor camps and the growing cities put further pressure on peasant agriculture.

Attempts by Chewa farmers to grow tobacco and corn for export were crushed by unfair taxation and the destruction of their crops. British farmers disliked competing with the Chewa and tried every method possible to force them out of business. Farm land for individual families

The Chewa were expert farmers, but they lost most of their land during colonization. Seen here are some of the items used in growing and preparing food, including a hoe, baskets, a pestle and mortar, and several upturned pots.

became scarce. Overpopulation began to damage the countryside.

Mission schools offered a way out of the problems of rural life. Mission education qualified Africans for positions as teachers, bureaucrats, police, foremen, clerks, and translators in the new economy. These people took charge when Malawi became independent.▲

chapter

7

THE CHEWA IN MODERN MALAWI

DURING WORLD WAR II, AFRICANS FROM British colonies fought together as members of the British Empire. Despite their different backgrounds, Africans shared similar experiences at war. They realized that their experience of colonization was also similar. Having witnessed the atrocities committed by Europeans during the war, Africans saw that the moral superiority that many whites claimed was wrong. After the war, a brief period of resistance to colonialism united Africans. Within two decades, most British colonies in Africa freed themselves of the colonizers.

After World War II, ethnic rivalries in Malawi were put aside in the push for independence. Over the years, migrant miners to South Africa had also built unity among themselves as Malawians, rather than as separate ethnic groups.

In 1964 Dr. Hastings Kamuzu Banda became the first president of independent Malawi. He single-handedly controlled Malawi until 1993.

Banda had lived in South Africa and had received his doctorate in medicine in the United States. His vision was for Malawi to become a fully modernized country. Unfortunately, the methods Banda used were not democratic, progressive, or fair.

Two months after independence, in the Cabinet Crisis, Banda dismissed most of those who had helped him gain office. A year later he was the dictator of a one-party state. All opposition was crushed. Banda's opponents were imprisoned or even murdered. This pattern of oppression continued throughout Banda's rule. In 1971, Banda declared himself President for Life. Banda owned controlling shares in most of the big companies in Malawi. Only his friends were given opportunities to enrich themselves.

Unlike other African leaders, Banda was prepared to deal with South Africa. South Africa was then ruled by the racist apartheid regime. Many ties were created between the two countries. South Africa paid for Banda to build a new capital at Lilongwe, in the heart of Chewa territory.

Like the apartheid government of South Africa, Banda used ethnic differences to divide the people and strengthen his position. A Chewa himself, Banda set out to give power to other Chewa. He also created the false idea that Malawi was solely a Chewa country. However, publicly he opposed tribalism.

First, Banda replaced the official language of Tumbuka with ChiChewa and English. Tumbuka was banned from the radio. Because mission schools had taught in Tumbuka, Tumbuka-speakers held most positions in administration and government. Banda selected Chewa bureaucrats to replace them.

Standardized tests for entrance to higher education were made more difficult in non-Chewa regions. This resulted in more graduates and opportunities for Chewa people. Banda's government removed non-Chewa from university and government posts during the 1970s, calling this "affirmative action." While education in Malawi suffered, Banda built an elite high school called the Kamuzu Academy. Here selected pupils were taught conservative ideas, including what people should be allowed to wear. Under Banda, bell-bottoms and short skirts were banned.

Banda manipulated Chewa history to suit his own ends. He promoted the idea that all people culturally related to the Chewa are in fact Chewa. Even the Lomwe, refugees from Mozambique, were labeled "Chewa" in the 1966 census. By claiming that other peoples were Chewa, Banda's MCP was able to claim a Chewa

majority in Malawi. Some scholars who supported Banda even claimed that the Maravi were
really the Chewa. Banda angered Malawi's
neighbors by demanding that Chewa areas in
present-day Zambia and Mozambique should
belong to Malawi.

Banda tried to use the Nyau Society as a
political weapon. During the Cabinet Crisis,
Nyau members intimidated Banda's opponents.
Similarly, he used the League of Malawi Women,
or "Banda Women," as a support group for his
personal power. He mobilized the youth in the
Young Pioneers, which educated rural people in
the "correct" use of ChiChewa. Despite Banda's
emphasis on Chewa tradition, women and traditional leaders lost power under the Banda
regime.

Malawi's economy suffered under Banda. In
1992 international aid to Malawi was stopped
because of human rights violations.

On June 14, 1993, the people of Malawi
voted for an end to Banda's one-party state.
Bakili Muluzi was elected president on May 19,
1994. In 1995 the aged Dr. Hastings Kamuzu
Banda was put on trial for the murder of political rivals back in 1983.▲

chapter

8

CEREMONIES

IN THE CITIES AND VILLAGES OF MALAWI, visitors will notice elements of contemporary life that are seen throughout the world. The traditions and ceremonies of Chewa culture continue in ways that have adjusted to the needs of the present.

Initiation ceremonies and masked dances are important links to the past. These ceremonies also comment on today's conditions. The symbolism of fire, ash, rain, and fertility remain important. The distinction between civilized behavior and wildness is also vital.

▼ CINAMWALI ▼

Cinamwali is the initiation of girls into the proper behavior expected of women and mothers. To receive the secret knowledge of Cinamwali, the girls are secluded for several weeks in a special initiation house. They are taught by a senior woman in the lineage who specializes in women's matters and the Chewa values that apply to them. Called the Namkungwi, she teaches the girls medical, sexual, spiritual, and symbolic matters known only to women. One of the symbolic ideas they learn is that women are like the sacred antelope which is hunted by men. Much of Cinamwali teaching occurs through special songs and dances. Such rites are performed wearing cloth masks.

In the past, clay figures in the form of animals and pottery vessels were used to communicate Cinamwali ideas. They were decorated with dots in red, white, and black. These are the colors of the python. The python is called the messenger of God and is said to ensure rainfall and fertility. Women are still painted with these colored dots of the python when they return home from initiation (see the picture on page 34). These markings indicate their readiness to bear children. Today, very little about Cinamwali is known to outsiders.

▼ THE NYAU SOCIETY ▼

During the Maravi federation, the Nyau Society united men across the divisions of families, clans, villages, and chiefdoms. It was also a kind of political pressure group that kept the power of matrilineal groups and chiefs in check. The Nyau were scorned by missionaries

The masquerades of the men's Nyau Society have a long history. They have often played a political role. These Nyau dancers are from Malawi (top) and Zambia (bottom).

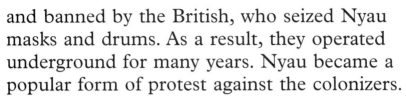

and banned by the British, who seized Nyau masks and drums. As a result, they operated underground for many years. Nyau became a popular form of protest against the colonizers.

After independence, Banda made Nyau dances a kind of official art form of Malawi. The dances were used to entertain officials, state visitors, and tourists. By pushing Nyau into public view, Banda used it for his own purposes. Nyau's traditional role of criticizing abuses of power was censored. Some prominent members of Nyau were publicly "unmasked." Others were imprisoned.

Today, nearly all Chewa men who are not strict Christians are members of Nyau. The Nyau Society is in charge of the secrets of men's initiation. It also performs elaborate masked ceremonies at the end of boys' initiation schools, at funerals of important persons, and at the installation of chiefs.

Chiefs are the organizers and controllers of secret initiation sites (*manda*). Unlike the women's initiation house, the *manda* is usually a graveyard hidden deep in the bush. The *manda* is forbidden to women. In the past, teenage boys spent several months or years learning the secret knowledge and proper conduct of men. Today the age of initiates is about eight or ten years old. Initiation may take only a few days. Boys initiated into Nyau together form strong bonds of friendship with each other that last a lifetime. After initiation, members of Nyau meet regularly in the *manda* to tell stories and share problems.

At initiation, Chewa boys are insulted and beaten by their teachers. Through this humiliation and their removal from the village to the wild space of the bush, the boys are symbolically "killed." They no longer belong to the world of women and girls. It is explained that young women, like the antelope, are to be pursued by men, who are "hunters." The boys are told to move out of their mother's house when they return to the village. They live with other bachelors until they marry.

Initiates are shown that Nyau masks are really men, and not spirits to be feared. They sacrifice a chicken and make their first mask. The initiates are "born" again into the world of men and into the Nyau Society. When the initiates finally return to the village from the bush school, the Nyau masked dances are staged. These graduation festivities occur at harvest time. Women brew large quantities of beer for the feast. Wearing costumes made of cloth, fiber, and wood, Nyau members masquerade as wild beasts and spirits, *zilombo*, from the bush. Everyone is present: men and women, chiefs and commoners, humans and ancestral spirits.

The Nyau festival dramatizes the world from the Chewa point of view. All aspects of the world outside of the village, including foreigners, spirits, animals, and the modern state are considered wild, alien, or not-human, *azungu*. Nyau dances also express ideals of gender, age, and rank.

The human identity of masked dancers is supposedly known to men only; women and children believe (or pretend to believe) that the masqueraders are real spirits. Although there are many different masquerade characters, they are all considered "wild spirits." Some come into the village to steal food, harass men, or make rude gestures to women.

▼ NYAU SYMBOLISM ▼

It is said that long ago men lived solely by farming. Men, spirits, and animals lived peacefully together. One day man accidentally invented fire, setting all the grasslands alight. God, the spirits, and all the animals ran from the fire. Men began hunting animals for food, and from then on, humans and animals were no longer friends. Humans could only rejoin God by dying so that they could follow Him. This story is linked to the annual fires that engulf the countryside at the end of the dry season. It is believed that the smoke from these fires rises up to become the clouds that bring rain. With the rain, ancestral spirits return to the earth, ensuring fertility for the next harvest. At hill shrines officials light ceremonial fires each year to call the rains and the ancestral spirits back to earth.

Nyau masqueraders, which appear at important moments in village life, are believed to be the animals and spirits returning to the world of humans. Some dancers represent predators and game animals. Predators are day beasts that hunger for food and thirst for beer, while night beasts are game animals (*nyama*) traditionally pursued by hunters.

Other Nyau appear as the spiritual counterparts of people from everyday life. Sometimes they appear as clowns who poke fun at Westerners or other characters from outside the village. A common comic character is "Simoni" (Simon Peter), who dances about in brightly colored pajamas, causing great laughter. "Maria" teaches proper sexual conduct by bad example. "Galimoto" is a huge, car-shaped basket that represents the motor car. In some villages, President Banda appears as "Kamuzu the Warrior," a dancer who threatens villagers until they hand over money. Although amusing, such characters have moral messages to present. Members of the audience understand the messages differently depending on their level of knowledge (*adziwa*).

Dancers follow each other in procession into the village. The most important masks are large basketry constructions, made of grass and maize leaves. These masks represent sacred animals such as the elephant or antelope. Called Nyau

A comic character in Nyau masquerades is "Simoni." This performance was held in Mkaika, Zambia, in 1985.

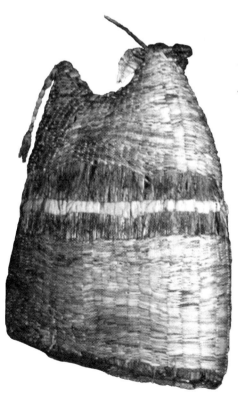

The most important masks are giant baskets that represent sacred animals. Seen here are two masks called Kasiya Maliro, which appear at funerals.

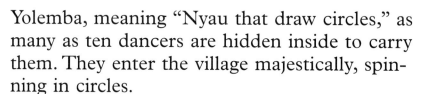

Yolemba, meaning "Nyau that draw circles," as many as ten dancers are hidden inside to carry them. They enter the village majestically, spinning in circles.

Sometimes a funeral coincides with men's graduation. When this occurs, a mourning ceremony, called *bona*, is combined with the graduation. A special Nyau Yolemba, known as Kasiya Maliro (the eland), appears toward the end of festivities, late at night. Kasiya Maliro means "that which abandons mourning" because it is the eland that dances in front of the dead person's house after the funeral. After performing this dance, the eland returns to the bush with the deceased's spirit. In the bush, Kasiya Maliro is burned. The Nyau initiates eat the ashes of the mask. This makes them immune to the dangerous "heat" that spirits are believed to have. The death of an elder is thus tied to the symbolic "birth" of the young initiates. Through Nyau ceremonies, elder men "give birth" to young adult men, paralleling the way that women give birth to infants.

The coming of the eland to the village and its return to fire in the bush echo important symbols in the Chewa view of creation and the renewal of life. These Chewa symbols are the fire and ashes connected to rain and fertility, and the return of animals and spirits to the world to mourn together with humans. ▲

Glossary

bona Ceremony celebrating the harvest.

Cinamwali Secret initiation school for girls.

controlling shares Having decision-making power over a business.

eland The largest of the African antelopes.

lineage Persons related to the same ancestor.

malambo Valleys that flood during the rains.

manda Secret initiation sites for men.

matrilineage System in which descent and inheritance follow the female line.

mbumba Family group, related to a senior mother, which shares a household.

MCP Malawi Congress Party.

Namkungwi Older woman who runs Cinamwali and advises women and chiefs.

ndiwo Spicy vegetable stew served with meals.

nkhoswe Mother's elder brother who is responsible for the well-being of the family.

nsima Stiff porridge made of corn or sorghum.

Nyau Society The men's secret association.

oral history Stories told by people about their past.

tribute Items given to a chief by his subjects.

For Further Reading

Birch Faulkner, Laurel. "Basketry Masks of the Chewa." *African Arts*, Vol. 21, May, 1988, pp. 28–31.

Crosby, Cynthia A. *Historical Dictionary of Malawi*, 2d ed. London: Scarecrow Press, 1993.

O'Toole, Thomas. *Malawi in Pictures*. Minneapolis: Lerner, 1988.

Yoshida, Kenji. "Masks and Secrecy Among the Chewa." *African Arts*, Vol. 26, April, 1993, pp. 34–45.

CHALLENGING READING

Alpers, Edward A. *Ivory and Slaves: Changing Pattern of International Trade in East Central Africa to the Later Nineteenth Century*. Berkeley: University of California Press, 1975.

Pachai, B., ed. *The Early History of Malawi*. Evanston: Northwestern University Press, 1972.

Index

ABOUT THE AUTHOR
John Peffer-Engels received a bachelor's degree in African Studies from the Individualized Major Program at Indiana University, and a master's degree in Art History from Columbia University. He has conducted research in South Africa on a Fulbright grant and is currently writing a doctoral dissertation on art schools in the South African townships.

PHOTO CREDITS
Cover, pp. 8, 12, 14, 17, 20 top, 20 bottom, 23, 29, 30, 42, 44, 46, 53 top, by Laurel Birch de Aguilar; pp. 34 top, 34 bottom, 58, 59 top, 59 bottom, by Kenji Yoshida, Ph.D., p. 53 bottom, courtesy of the Zambian Cultural Services/Elizabeth Ann Schneider, Ph.D.

EDITOR: Gary N. van Wyk, Ph.D.

LAYOUT AND DESIGN: Kim Sonsky

4/19